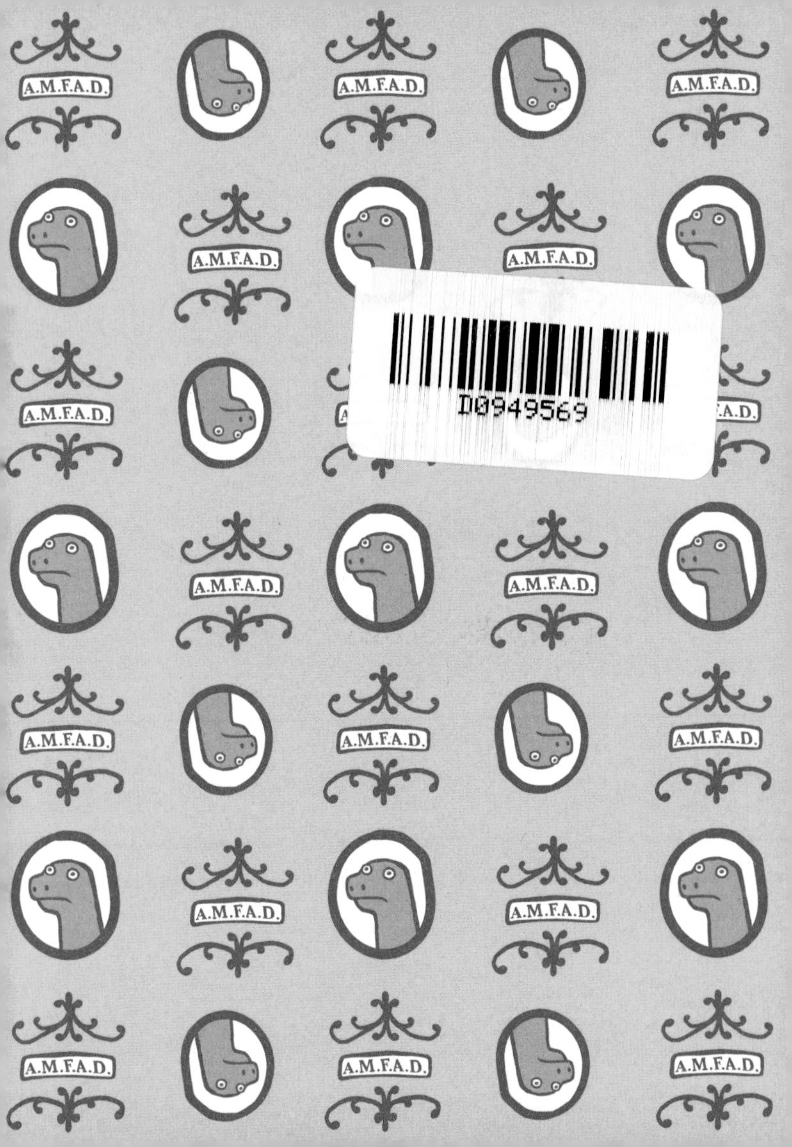
A.M.F.A.D.

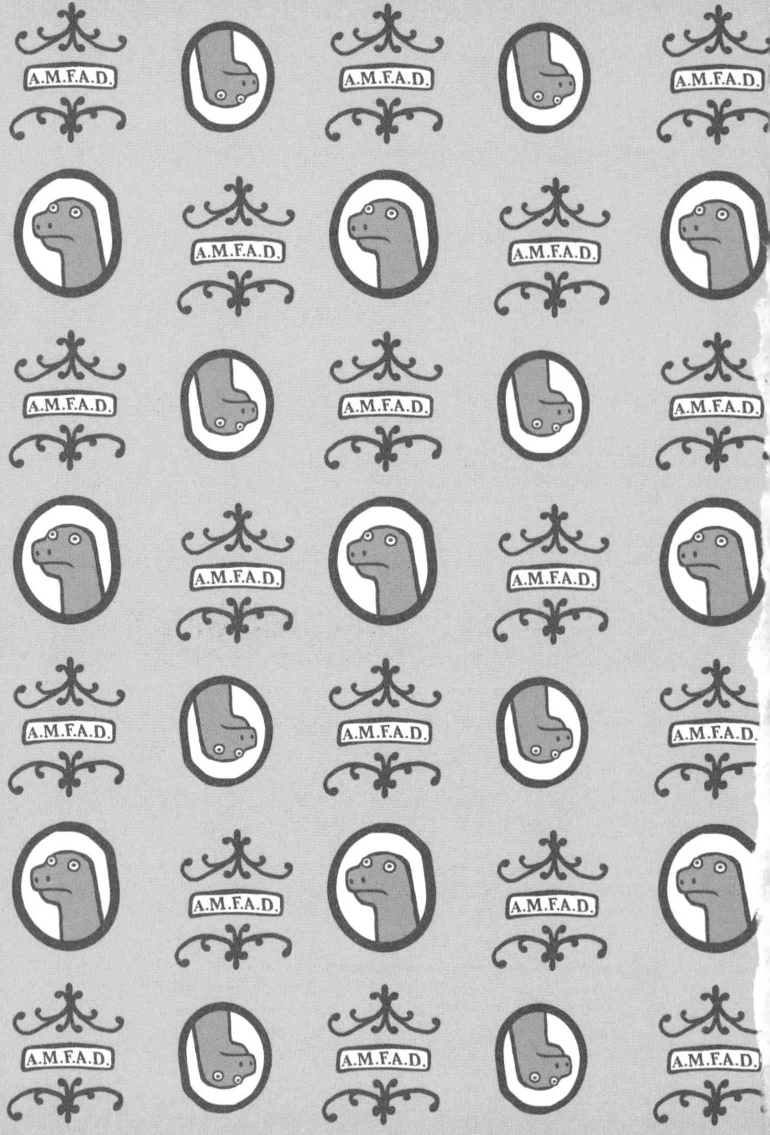
A.M.F.A.D.

All my
friends
are dead.

Library of Congress Cataloging-in-Publication Data is available.

ISBN: 978-0-8118-7455-7

Manufactured in China

Designed by Avery Monsen

10 9 8 7 6 5 4 3 2 1

Chronicle Books LLC
680 Second Street
San Francisco, California 94107
www.chroniclebooks.com

All my friends are dead.

Avery Monsen and Jory John

CHRONICLE BOOKS

SAN FRANCISCO

All my friends are dead.

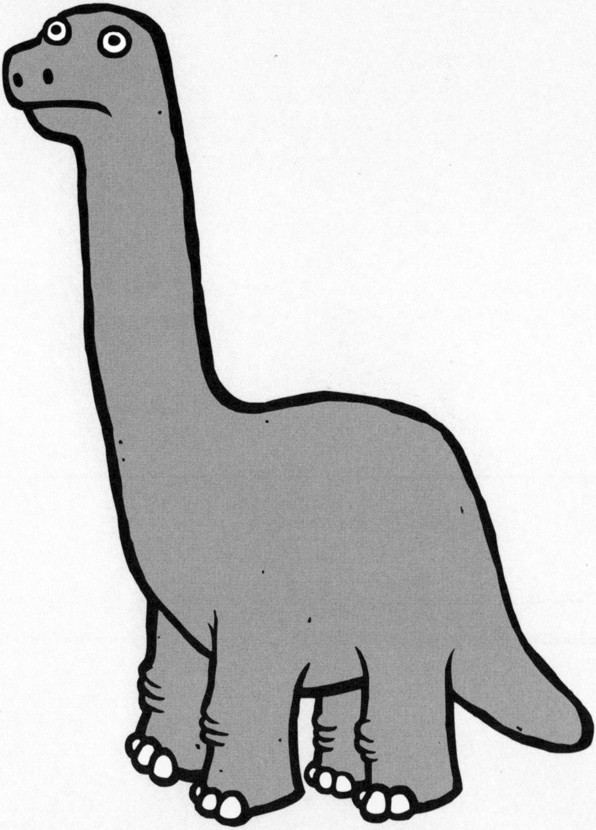

All *my* friends are dead.

Most of
my friends
are dead.

What?

Oh.

Now all
my friends
are dead.

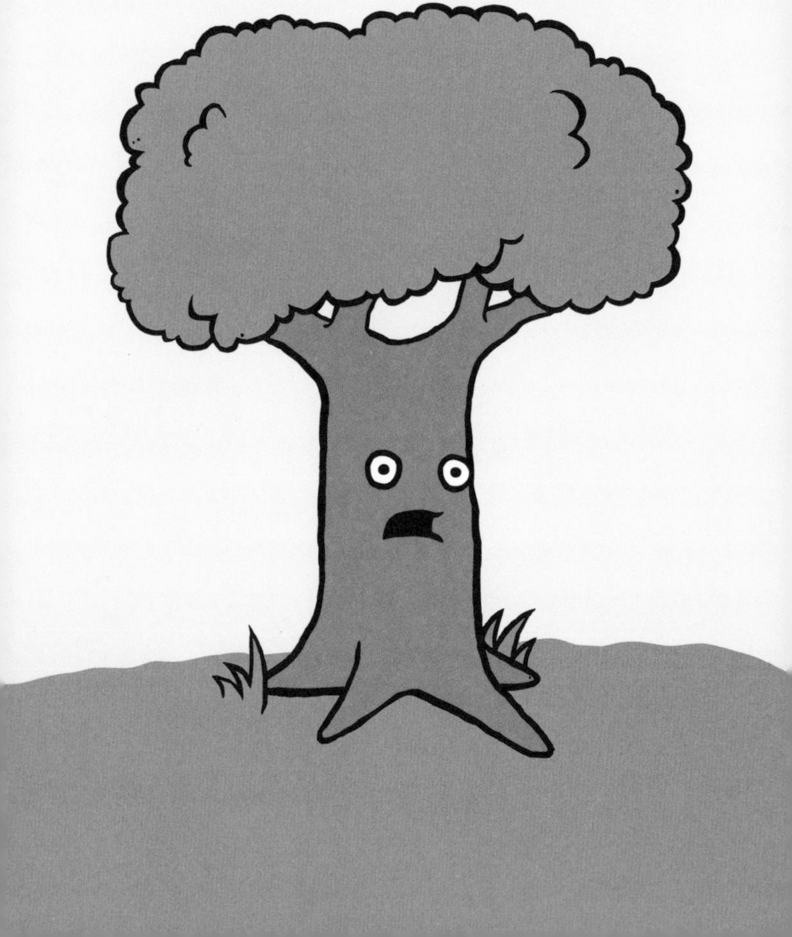

All my
friends are
end tables.

I was never friends with that guy.

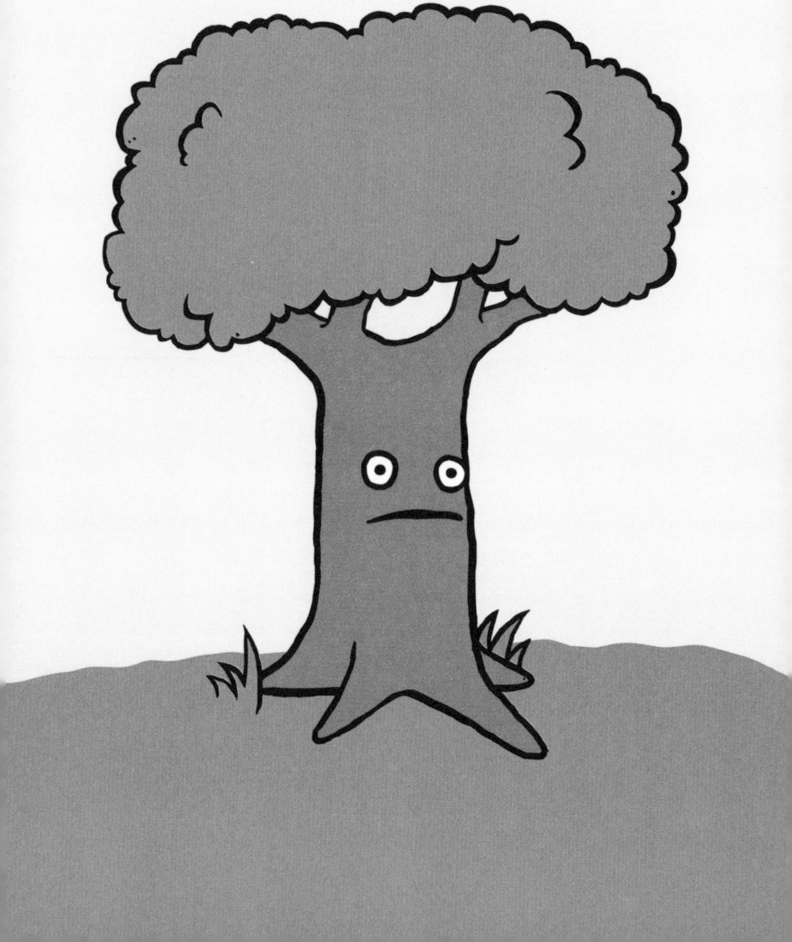

Dangit.

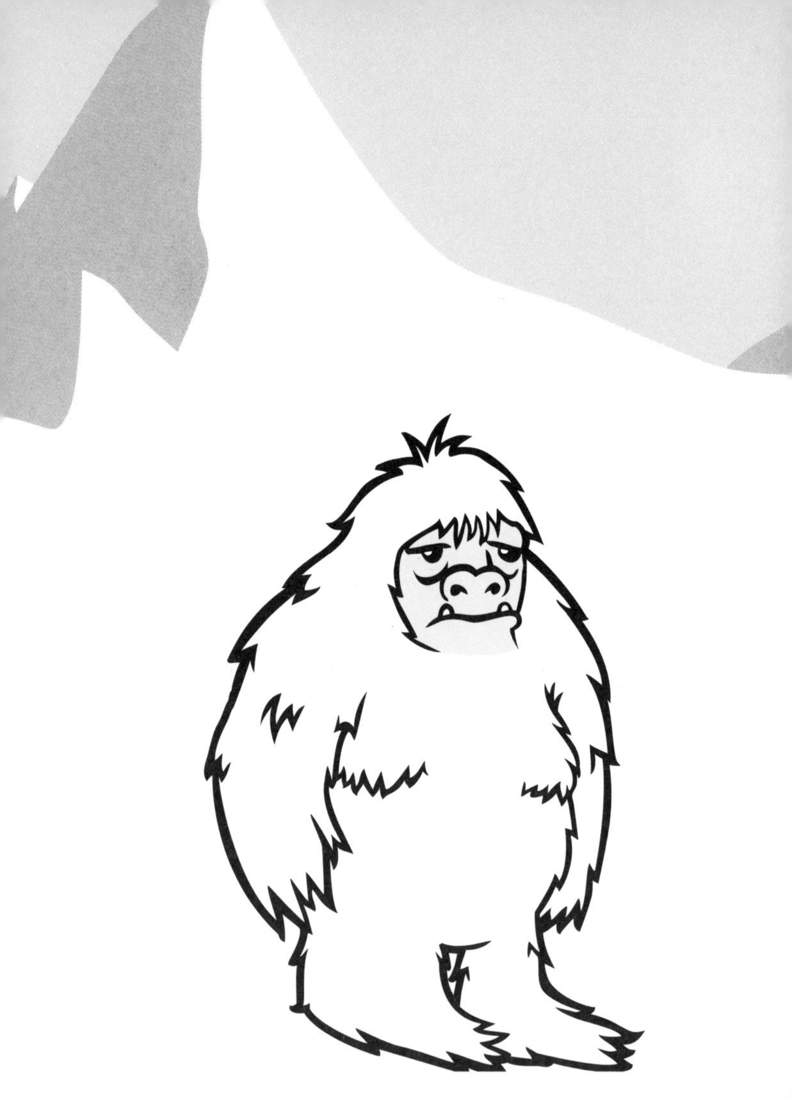

All my
friends are
hoaxes.

I sort of
resent that.

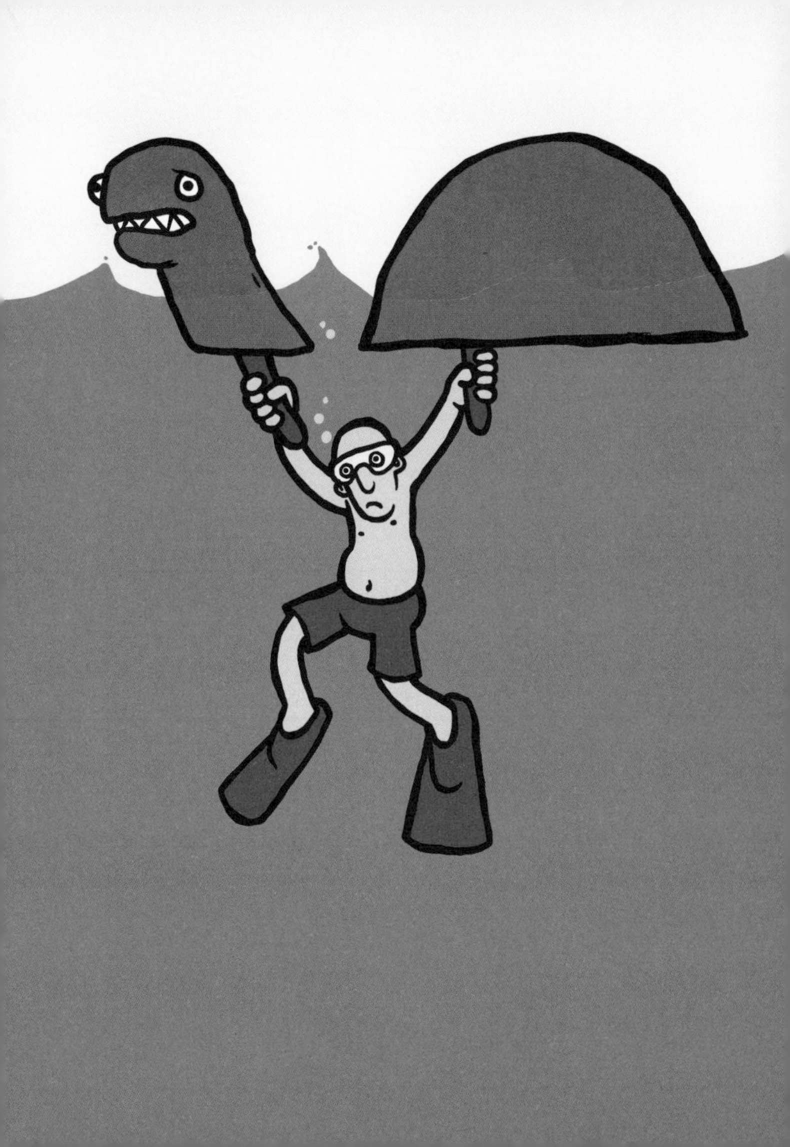

All my friends are *un*dead.

All my
friends
are bread.

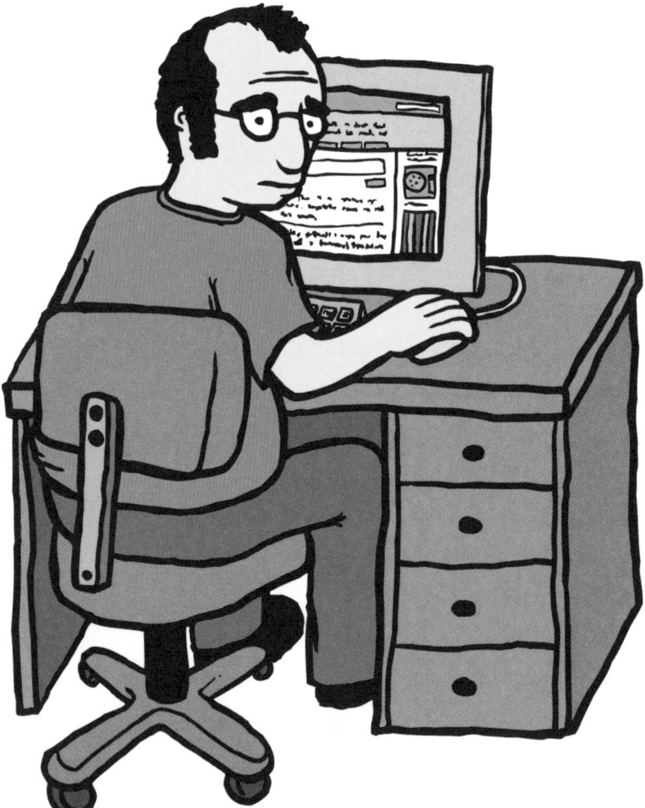

I have 3,284 friends.

I've just never met any of them face to face.

All my friends
are Phil!

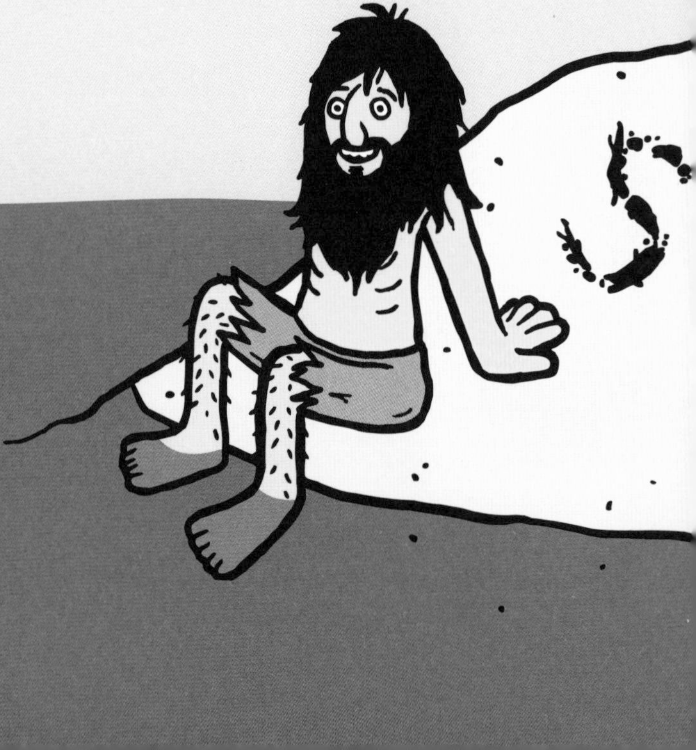

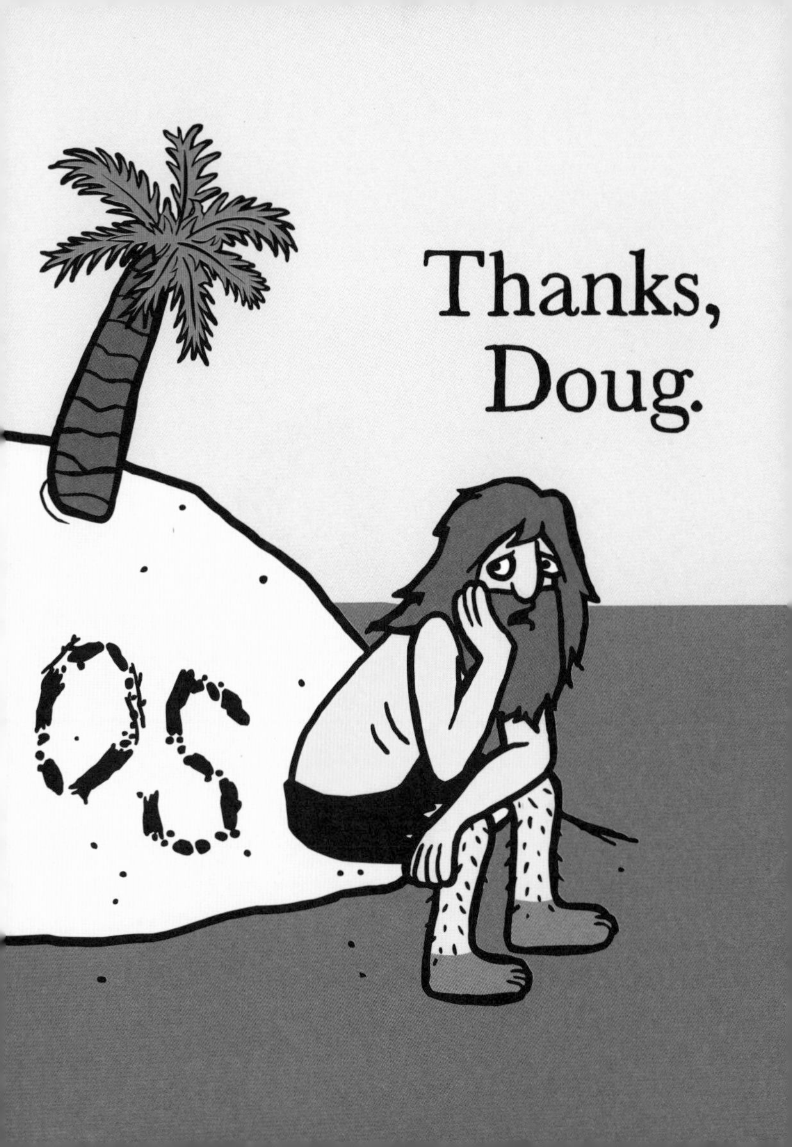
Thanks,
Doug.

The only ship we need is a *friend*-ship, huh, Phil?

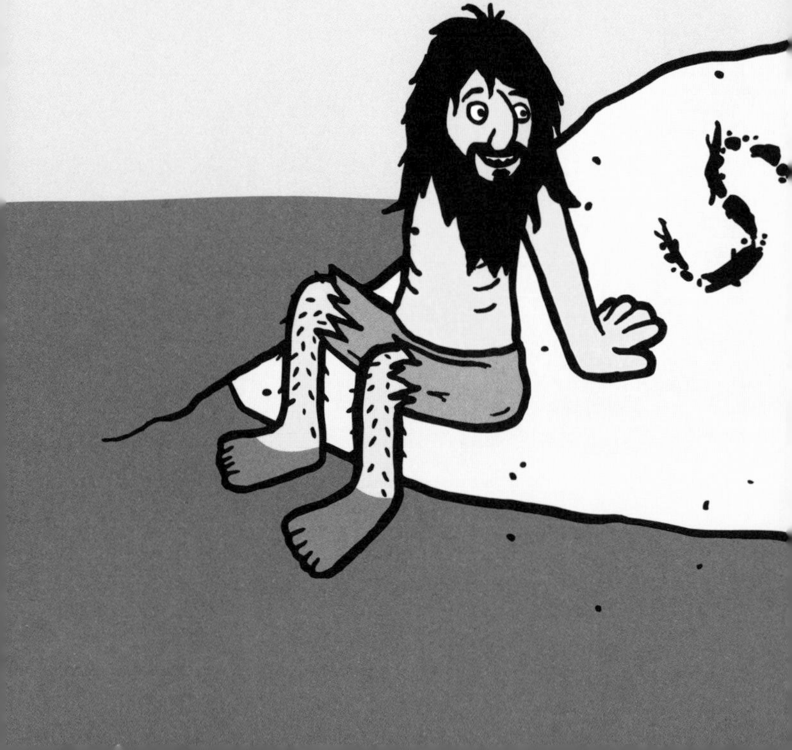

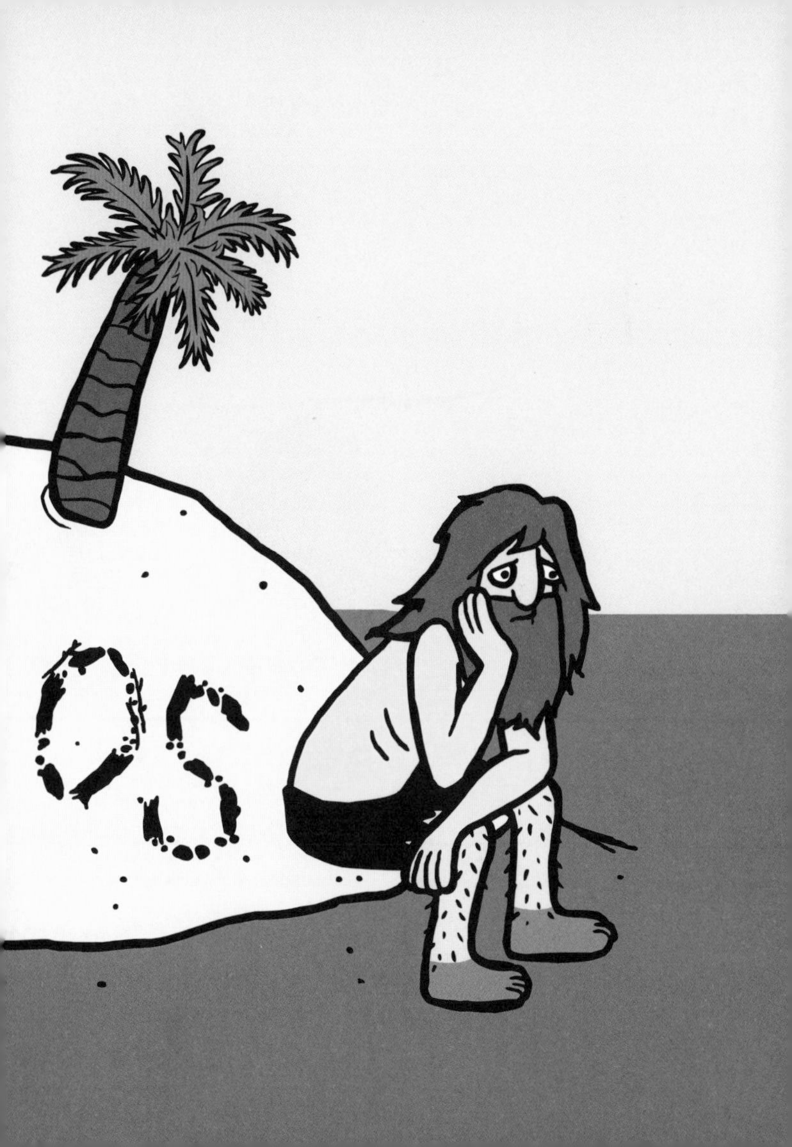
OS

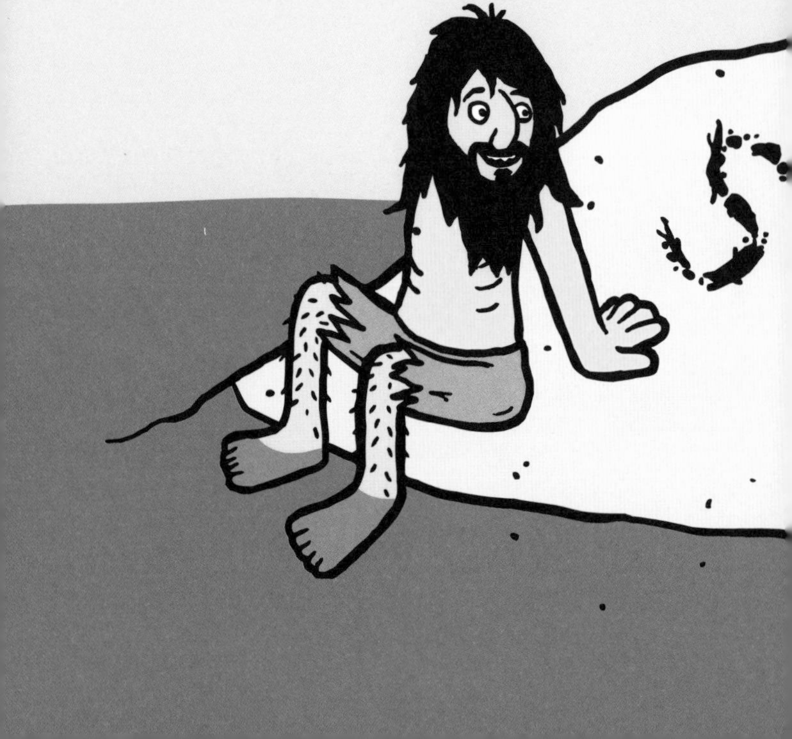

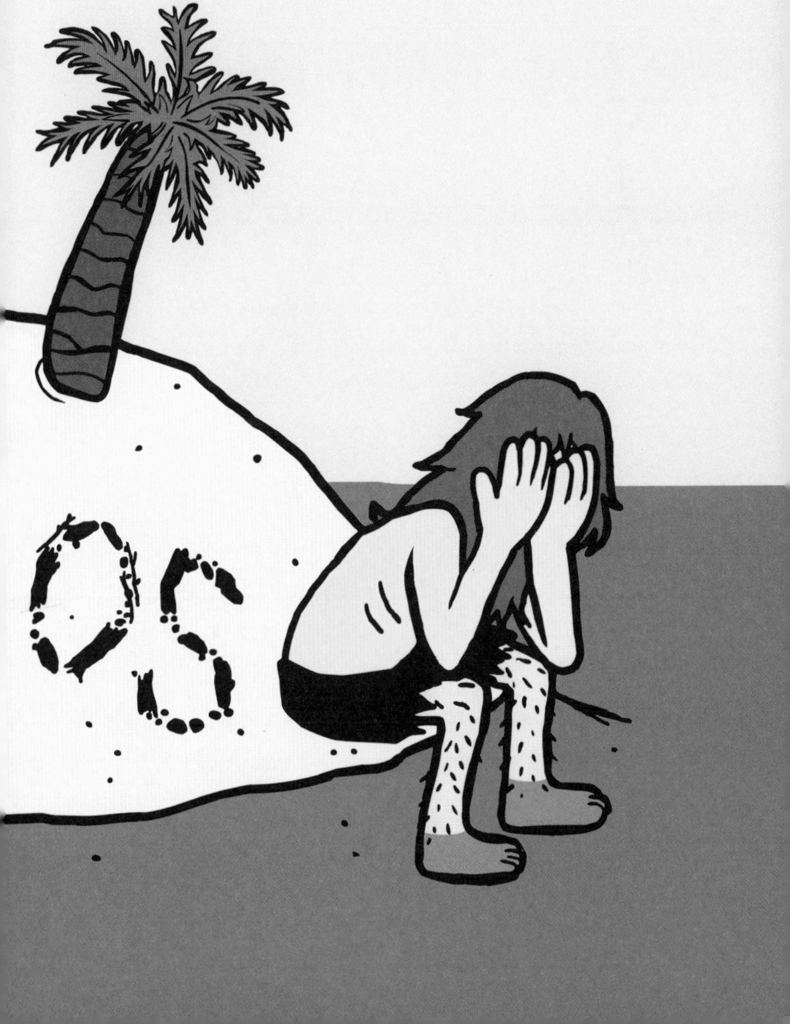
OS

Friendship.

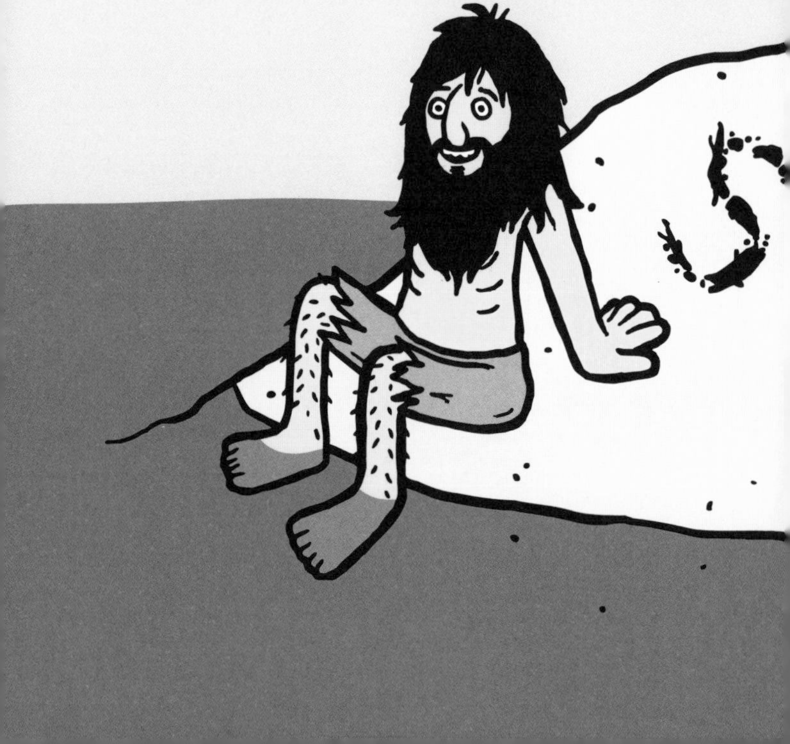

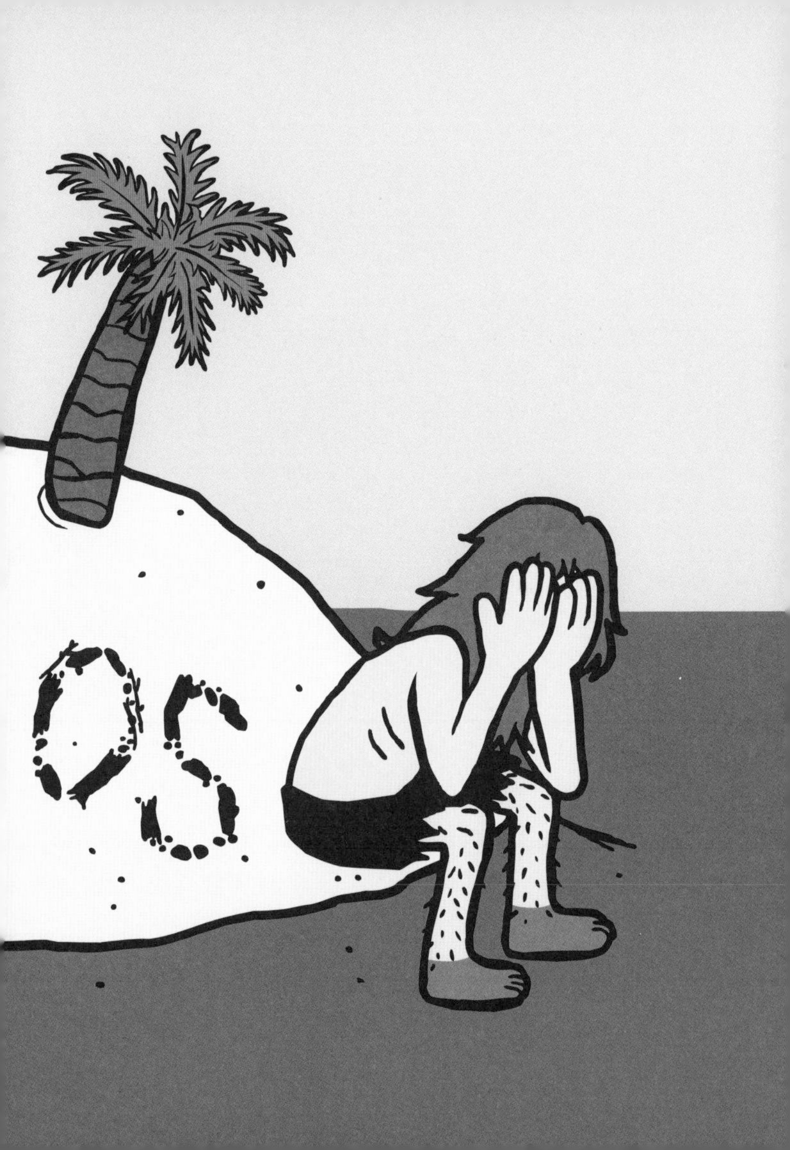
OS

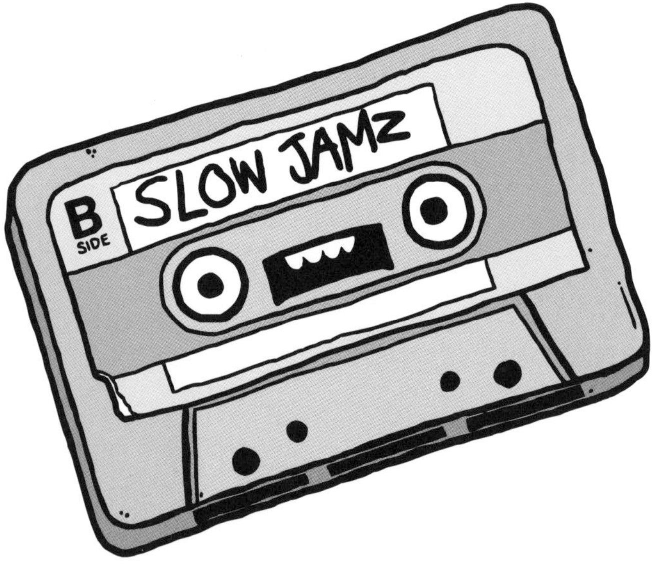
B
SIDE
SLOW JAMZ

All my friends are obsolete.

My only friend
has recently gone
missing.

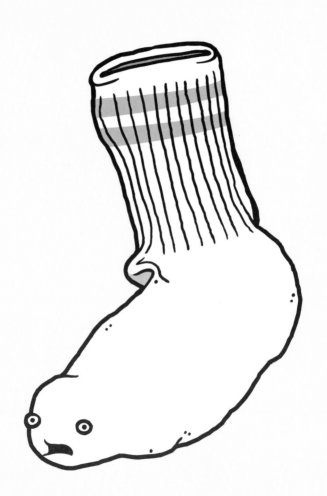

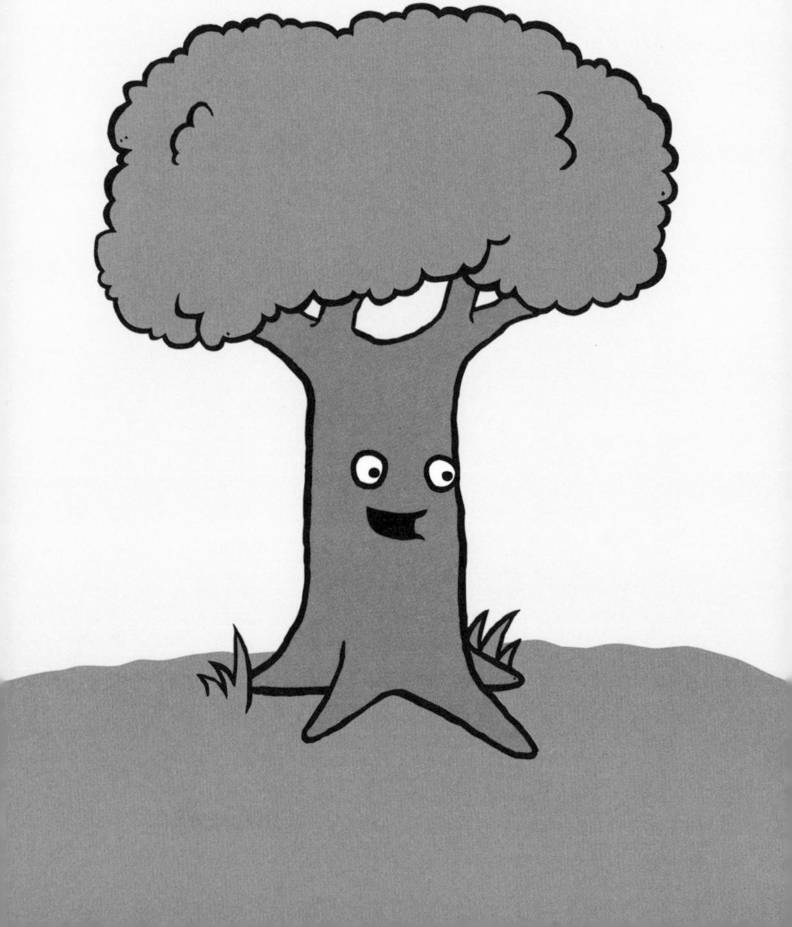

Hey there,
little fella!

Will you be
my friend?

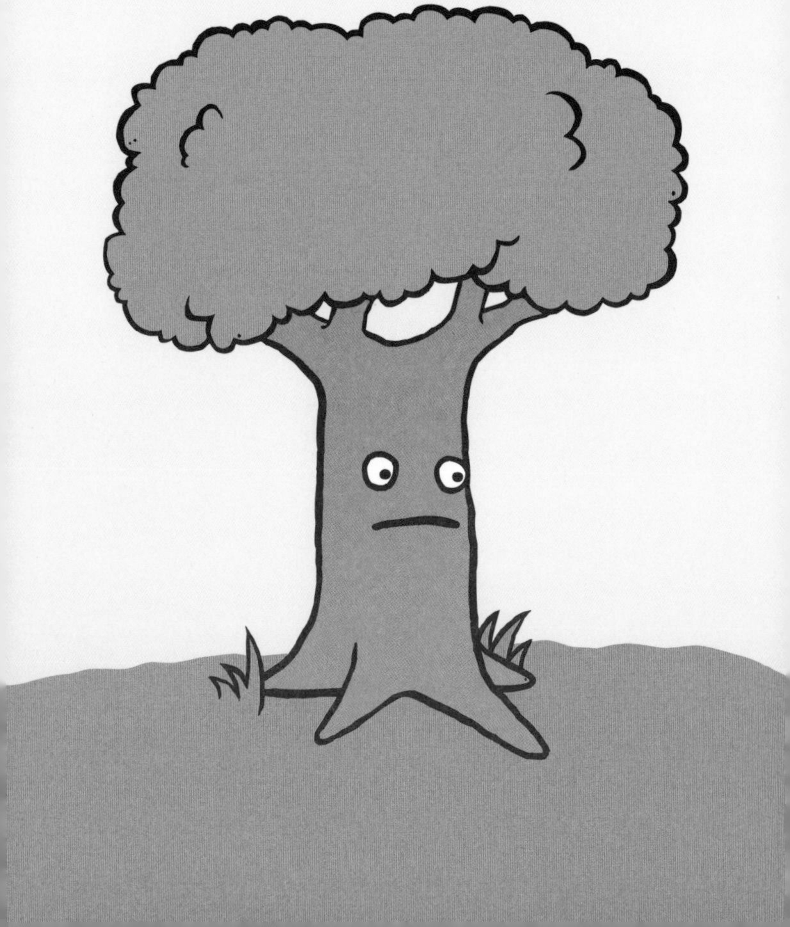

I'd rather not.
Carlos told me
you got mono.

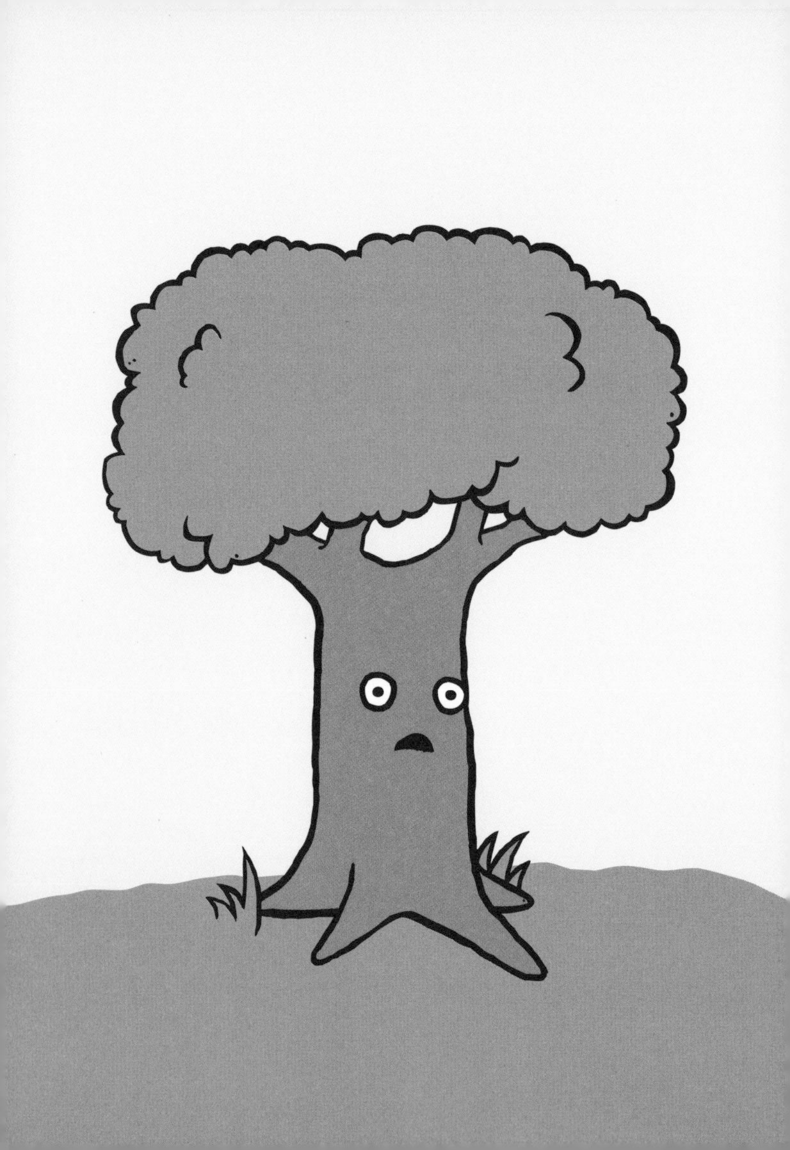

This is my
worst day.

2%
REDUCED FAT
MILK
ONE GALLON
EXP

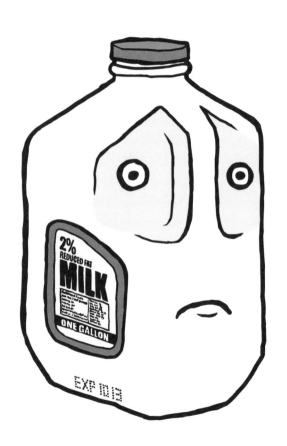

All my
friends
expired on
Tuesday.

All my friends
have scurvy.

Yarr.

All my friends are terrifying.

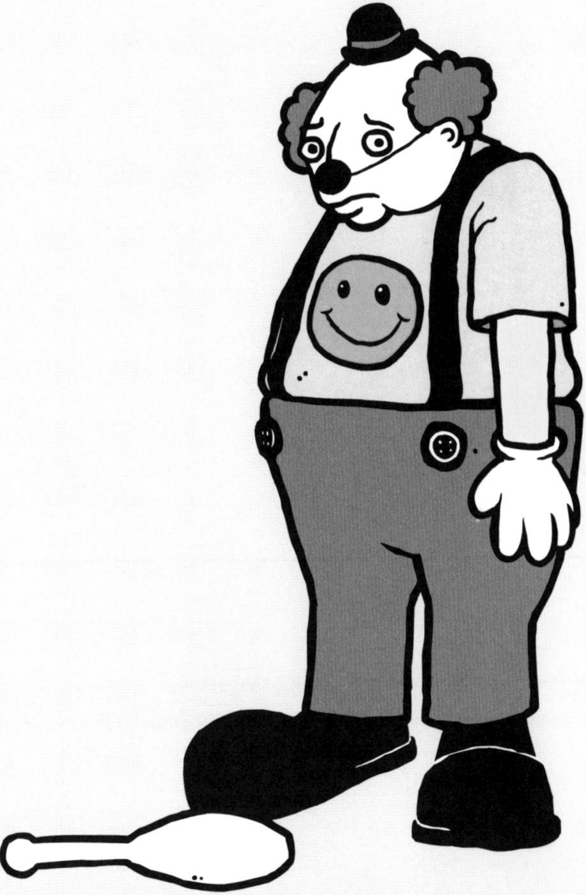

I've already made two children cry today!

All my
friends are
soooooooooooo
last season.

All my friends
are dummies.

All my friends
are puddles.

All my friends are Kentucky fried.

All your friends
are delicious.

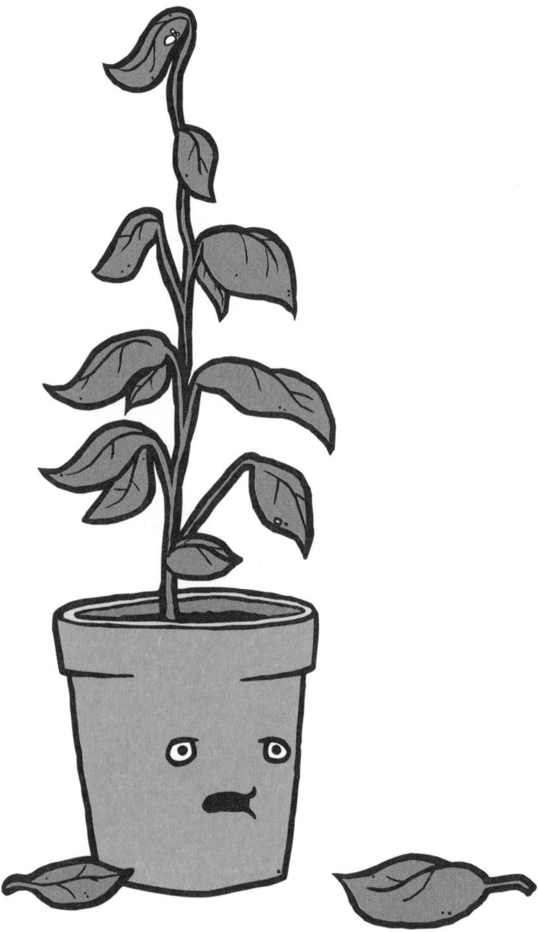

Please stop buying
my friends if you
are just going to
slowly kill them.

All my friends
are followers.

Where are we going?

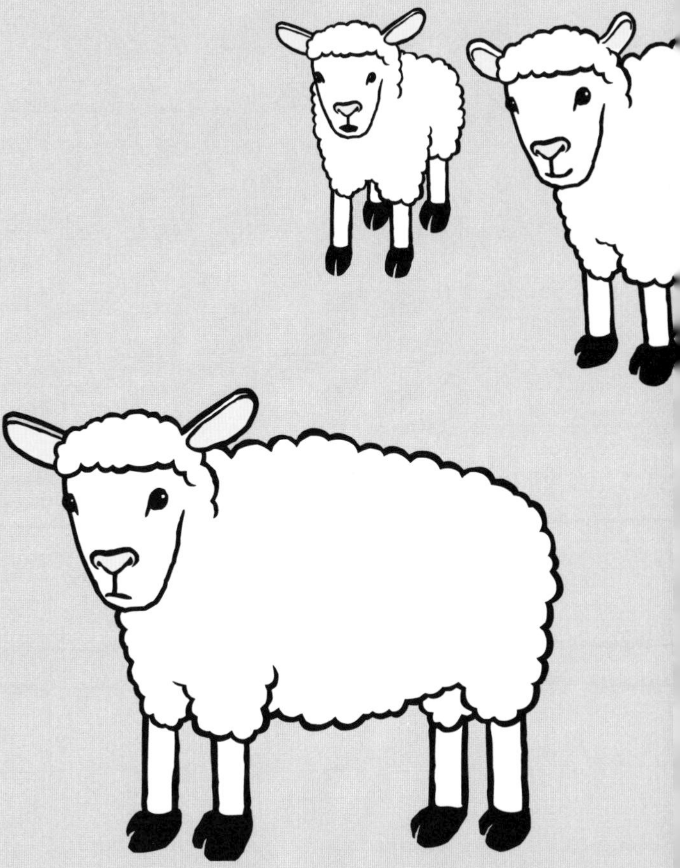

(None of my friends will speak to me.)

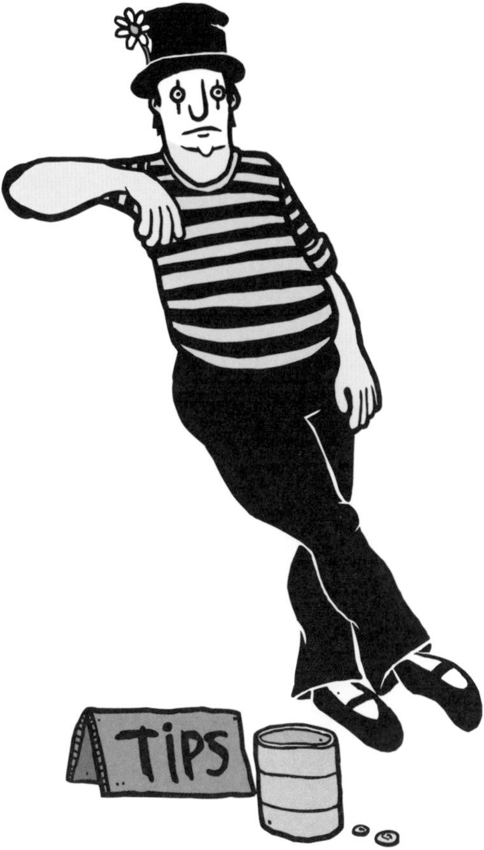
TIPS

All my friends
will be dead
within 24 hours.

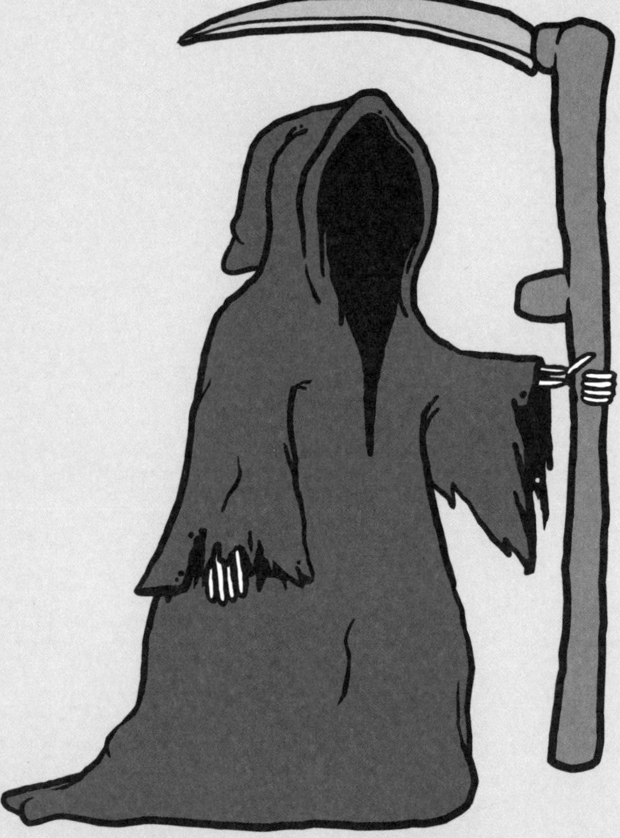

This job makes
me feel so alive.

Howdy.

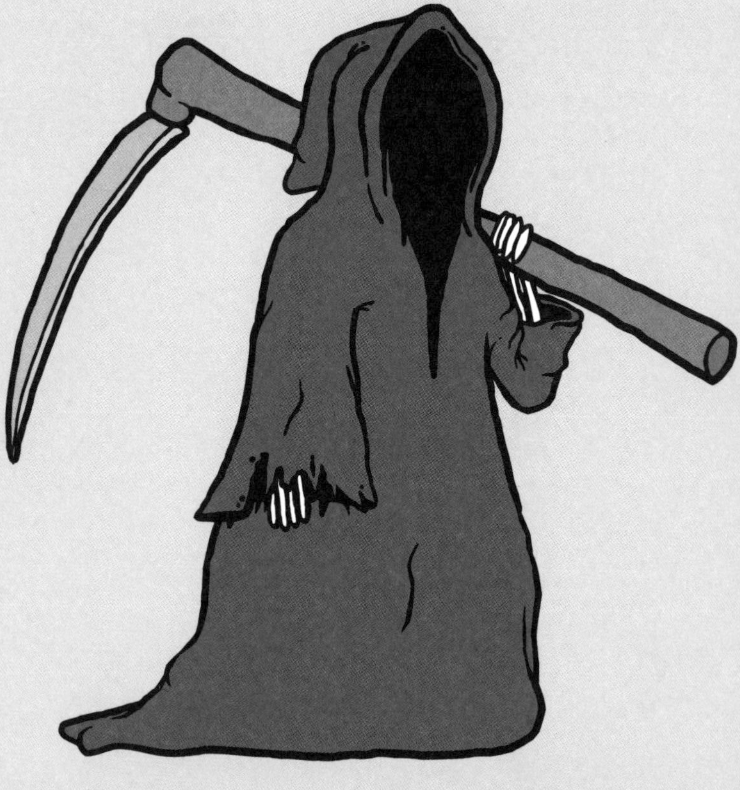

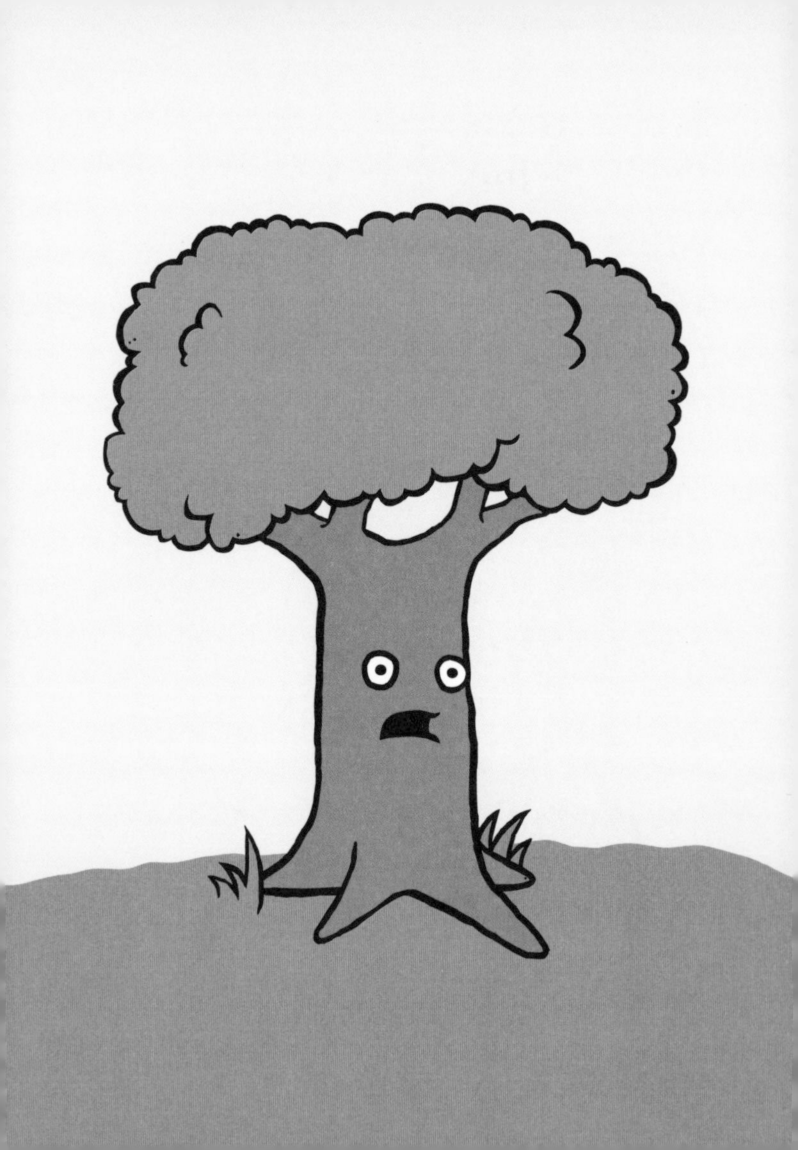

Sometimes I feel alone. Some days are long and hard. But when I look out into the world, I am struck by the impossible beauty of it all. Those billions of magnificent accidents that led us to where we are today, that led us to paper planes and nautilus shells and the tiny, crooked smiles of children. When I think about all the small perfections of the world, I have faith that my time will come. I have faith that someday, a warm light will flood over me and I will find peace.

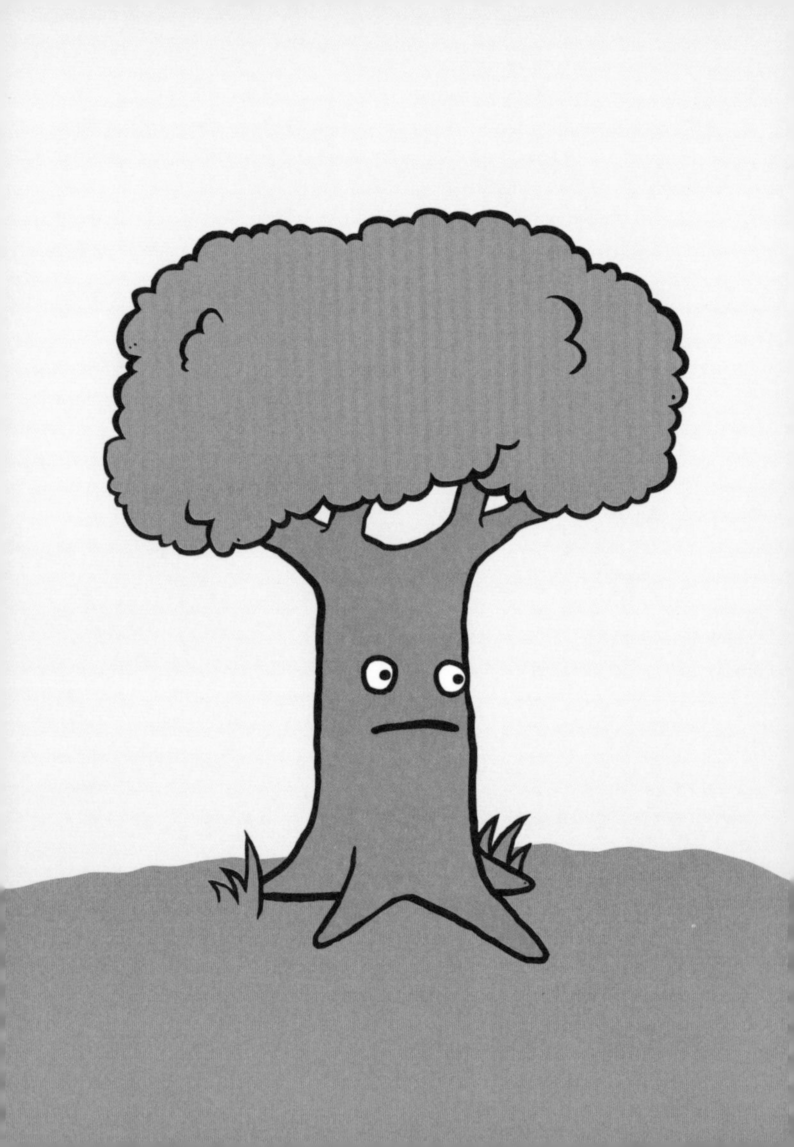

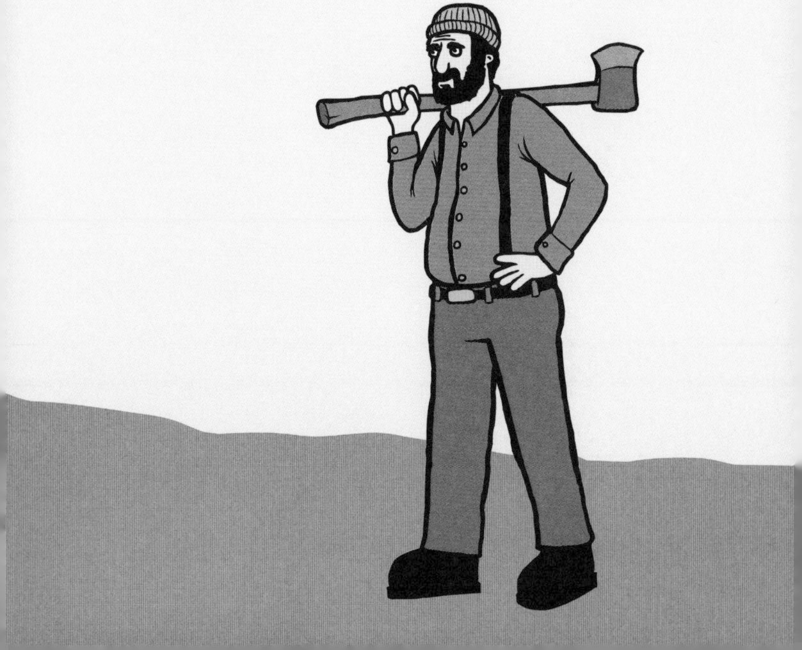

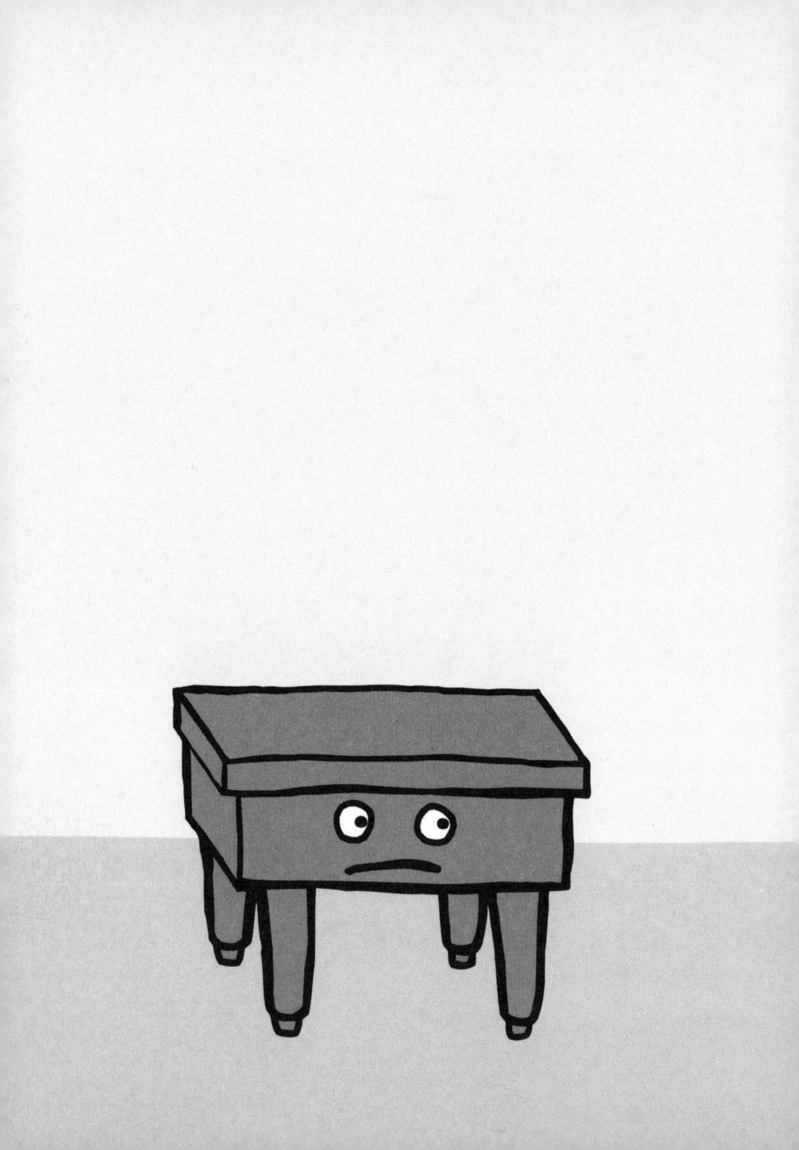

I'm still not
your friend.

Acknowledgments

Many thanks to everybody at Chronicle Books, especially Steve Mockus, Emilie Sandoz, Erin Thacker, and Suzanne LaGasa.

And our friends and families: Mac Barnett, SV Bliss, Zak Fishman, Emily Heller, Deborah John, James Keary, Clare McNulty, Bill Monsen, Risa Monsen, Gail Rubin, Monica Schaefer, Patrick Shaffner, Ben Sinclair, Jennifer Traig, and Lawrence Wilson.

About the Authors

Avery Monsen is an actor, artist, and writer.

Jory John is a writer, editor, and journalist.

They are the co-authors of *Pirate's Log: A Handbook for Aspiring Swashbucklers.*

They are friends. And neither is dead. Yet.

For more sad and funny things, visit
www.nomorefriends.net.

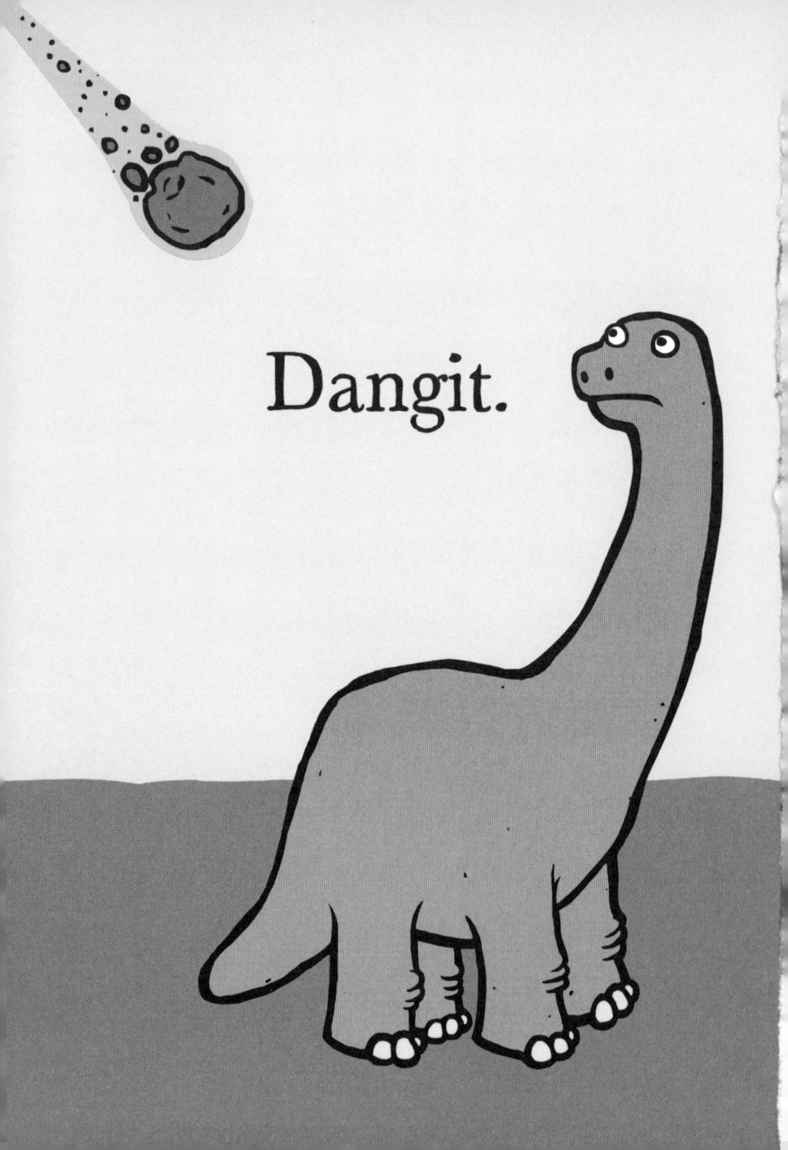
Dangit.

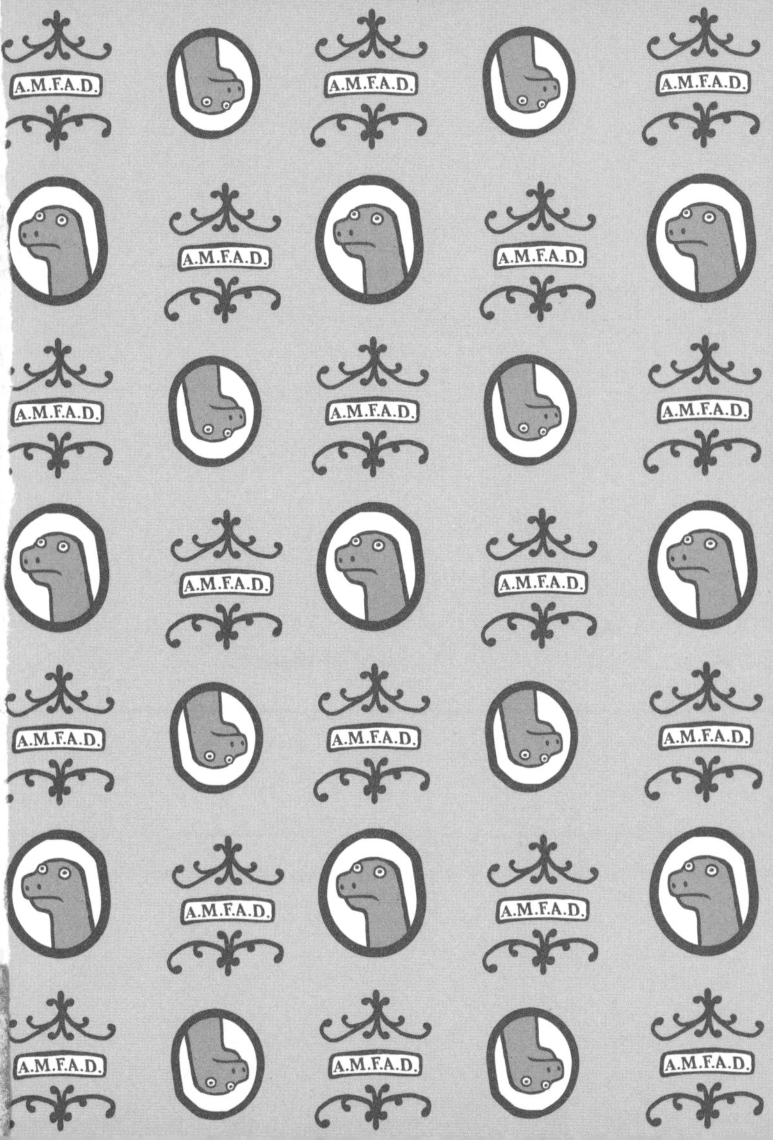
A.M.F.A.D.

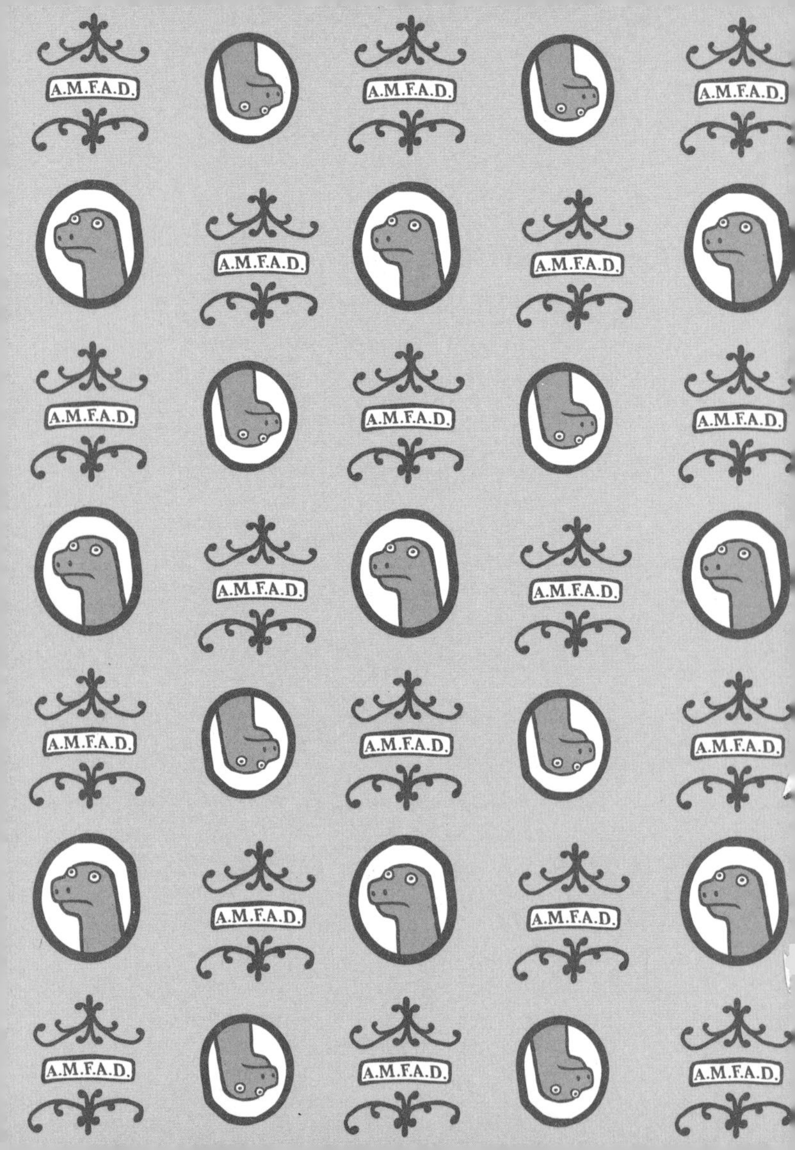
A.M.F.A.D.